How to Stay Alive on

By Steve C Holder

November 2017

Edition 1.2

I would like to thank Judith Stringer and Martin O'Connor who have helped with the editing and proof reading of this book.

With each copy of this book sold there is a free MP3 music track available called "Burning On". This rock track (written and performed by the author with guitar contributions from Jim Gorton) is from the 3 song album Indigo Road under the band name "The DryLandPirates".

To claim your free copy of the track "Burning on", e-mail hpbs86@gmail.com.The full album is available to buy on Amazon and other outlets. Rock on.

Foreword: This book provides a humorous insight into the different types of road users observed during my years of commuting as a biker. I have had very close encounters with all the characters set out in here! I hope that by recognising them and trying to anticipate what they might do it might save someone's life one day.

The insights are supported by data from the Office for National Statistics and the Department for Transport.

The characterisations are easy to remember and I have set out my own "Biker Response" that has kept my Yamaha Fazer F8 (with ABS) "shiny side up" to date. It will appeal to new or experienced bikers, concerned mums and car drivers alike.

I hope you enjoy the insights into Daddy's Little Girl, Exec Man, Hi-Viz-Vest Man and others. Spotting them can also be fun for the family on long journeys. I have included a score-sheet, with some rules to stop any cheating, if you decide to play!

If you are easily offended, or have had a sense of humour bypass, please do not read this book.

Contents

Introduction

Although I enjoyed riding bikes when I was younger, it was only when I was "born again" in 2002, following a divorce and a mid-life crisis, that I decided to get a steel steed and mount up once more.

The way my life turned out meant that long commutes became the norm. I needed something that could cut through the endless lines of traffic between Wakefield, Manchester and York and deal with the raging madness of the M62, M60, M6, A64 and A57. A Yamaha Fazer was the obvious solution.

The thrill of riding a motorbike can be hard to explain to someone who has never done it. For me, I get a complete sense of freedom and I have to say it is the one time in my life where I am thinking about nothing else, other than staying alive. It is almost like meditation. I feel like I am flying through the air and almost become unconscious of the machine itself. The exhilaration of the acceleration, the vulnerability, the sense of being at peace with myself, the power, the risk, the smell of the open air, the feel of the wind rushing past and yes, the rebellion.

There are many biker stories, hints and tips developed over time to stop accidents. However, one thing has always been true. Anticipating the move of the driver in front (or behind) is crucial to staying alive. There is of course the four point rule most bikers live by. Specifically:-

1. Expect the driver in front to be a total knob
2. Expect cars to pull out at junctions
3. Don't go out in the rain, snow or high winds
4. Expect the driver behind to be a total knob

However, although this four point rule is good basic guide, it is not enough. I have conducted a detailed study over a number of years of driver behaviour and analysed biker injury rates from the Office for National Statistics and the Department for Transport to help refine this approach.

From this work, I have been able to develop a set of driver characteristics and likely behaviours. To my surprise, it became apparent that very similar driving styles are exhibited by similar types of car, depending on driver age and the driver's lifestyle. By recognising these characters on the road it will help to give those precious extra moments for the biker (or anyone else) to prepare to react to the impending traffic situation and to shift the odds a little in the bikers favour.

Deaths by Road User Types and Other Stuff

Whatever way you look at it, if you are on a motorbike you are in a vulnerable group. So how bad is it? The table below is frightening.

Table 1 - Casualty rate per billion miles

Transport Type	Killed[1]	Killed or Seriously Injured[1]
Car Occupants	2	21
Pedestrians[2]	34	463
Pedal Cyclists	34	1036
Motor Cyclist	114	1789

1 Rates calculated using traffic figures based on 2013 figures

2 National Travel Survey data used to calculate pedestrian rates.

It is easy to see what the most dangerous form of transport is per miles completed, although this does not tell the full story. The numbers of motorcyclists killed or seriously injured shown in table 2 have decreased by 106 riders since 2010 and the overall trend is in the right direction but it is still too many.

Table 2 – Motorcyclists killed or seriously injured 2010 to 2015

Number of Motorcyclists killed or seriously injured						
Year	**2010**	**2011**	**2012**	**2013**	**2014**	**2015**
Total	347	317	278	246	283	241

Source: Office of National Statistics

Interestingly, as can be seen in table 3 overleaf using figures from 2015, as a proportion of the number of licensed vehicles on the road you are 5 times more likely to be injured on a motorcycle than in a car. It does seem bizarre using this ratio that you are nearly ten times more likely to be injured on a bus or coach than on a motorbike! Who knew?

Table 3 – Casualties as a proportion of the number of licensed vehicles on the road

Type of Road User	2015	2015	Calculated figure*
	Reported casualties by road user type, Great Britain	Licensed vehicles on the road	Casualties as a percentage of vehicles on the road
Car occupants	111,707	30,222,000	0.07%
Motorcycle users	19,918	1,314,000	0.35%
Bus and coach	4,626	146,000	3.25%
HGV	1,203	474,500	0.00%

Source: Department for Transport

*Courtesy of HPBS Ltd Chartered Accountants

Accidents by Days of the week

When analysing the number of accidents by days of the week it is important to remember that generally speaking, there are two categories of bikers[1].Those that use their bike to commute to work and those that enjoy a ride out on a Sunday. It is unusual to find people that do both, although I am sure they are out there.

I have summarised in table 4 below the mortality rates by days of the week; the more detailed data from the Department for Transport also shows the actual time of day of the casualty[2]. For bikers the most dangerous days of the week are Friday's and Sundays. There may be a number of reasons for this that we will explore throughout this book.

Table 4 - Reported killed or seriously injured casualties by day and road user type Great Britain, 2015.

Weekday	Pedestrians	Pedal Cyclist	M'cycle Users	Car Users
Monday to Thursday	3,083	2,048	2,985	4,476
Average per Day	771	512	746	1,119
Friday	926	512	833	1,301
Saturday	792	390	780	1,451
Sunday	547	389	809	1,414

Source: Department for Transport

1 I know I should be saying "Those that have had an accident and those that

2 Some bikers go out Saturday. The danger times are between 4 pm and 8 pm with an average casualty rate of 81 between these times annually. This compares with 67 on a Friday between the same times!

The final set of statistics I want to present shows the injuries by road type for 2015. This table shows the number of casualties for motorcycles and all other road users, where the vehicle type was recorded.

In total, there were nearly 20 times more casualties on non-motorway roads than on a motorway. If you are riding a motorbike this ratio goes up to more than 80 times! It also shows that more than 50% of biker accidents occur on "A" roads; the obvious inference is speed and corners don't mix, however, the figures are pretty stark.

Table 5 – Casualties by road type

Type of Road	Motorcycles	All other Identified Reported Vehicles	Total	Percentage that involve motorcycles
Motorway	275	12,406	12,681	2.17%
A Roads	12,328	105,452	117,780	10.47%
B Roads	2,965	27,157	30,122	9.84%
Other Roads	7,129	79,456	86,585	8.23%
Total	**22,697**	**224,471**	**247,168**	**9.18%**

There are lots of statistics about accidents involving motorcyclists, but very little I have found about the other roads users who have also been involved that contributed to the accident in the first place.

In an attempt to explain and understand these people I have provided my own (completely made up but I hope amusing) analysis and rationale for their behaviours. We all know "White Van Man", but I would like to introduce you "Daddy's Little Girl", "Exec Man"," Hi-Viz Vest man" and others. Have fun!

Disclaimer: These characterisations are purely fictitious and are not based upon anyone I have ever known alive or dead.

PLEASE NOTE: THESE CHARACTERISATIONS DO NOT APPLY TO EVERYONE WHO MAY SEEM TO FIT IN A CATEGORY! THIS IS A GUIDE FOR BIKERS TO HELP ANTICIPATE BEHAVIOURS AND SHIFT THEIR ODDS OF SURVIVAL. PERHAPS THE CHARACTERISATIONS MAY ALSO MAKE CERTAIN TYPES OF CAR DRIVERS **THINK BIKE!**

Having put the disclaimer in, I bet you can recognise at least one of these people!

If you think you might be one of them and enjoy this book, I humbly and respectfully ask you, when driving think about that biker behind or in front of your vehicle.

From reading this, you will now know what he or she is thinking about you. I hope you let them get safely home to their family.

Daddy's Little Girl

To cut to the chase, the easiest way to identify Daddy's Little Girl has been set out in the table below. However, this is not enough. Read on.

How to identify

Parameters	What to expect
Driver Age Range	17-22
Typical Car	Vauxhall Corsa 1.2, Fiat 500, Ford Fiesta, Vauxhall Astra
Colour	Red, White, Beige, Light Blue
Driving Style	Random, sudden changes of lane, no indication
Tell-tale signs	On the phone, headphones in, vanity mirror down
Danger Rating	*****

There are very few things more dangerous on the road to a biker than Daddy's Little Girl; she is usually found driving a red 1.2 Corsa, Fiesta or Fiat. These cars are highly manoeuvrable. Any gaps at all in the traffic queues, Daddy's Little Girl will be into it faster than a starving rat finding a prawn sandwich left outside the Savoy.

Personality Type

To understand Daddy's Little Girl you need to accept her priorities are, in order:-

1. How she looks
2. How she looks
3. What her friends think about how she looks
4. The boyfriend or (even worse), the potential boyfriend
5. What she is going to wear on the Friday/ Saturday night
6. The next song, what's app message or Facebook post coming up on her smartphone

I am sorry but it is just a fact and actually it is good news for the motorcyclist. Daddy's Little Girl spends so much time looking in her rear view mirror there is at least a 50:50 chance that she will see your glaring headlamps approaching. I say 50:50, as the rear view is angled so she can look at herself; the side mirrors are never used (for obvious reasons) and to her are just "car earrings".

The bad news is, if she has not seen you there is a very high chance her headphones will be in, listening to Justin Bieber or Ed Sheeran; the latter is the artist of choice if she more an "Alto" than a "Soprano"[3]. There is no chance of her hearing the deep rumble of your motorbike engine, (this includes 1300 Harley's revved up to red). Unfortunately it is not just bike engines she cannot hear.

An indication that Daddy's Little Girl is up ahead can be fleet of stationary ambulances, with sirens blaring and blue lights flashing, unable to get past.

Home Life

To gain an insight into the road antics of Daddy's Little Girl, you need to understand she can twist her old man around her little finger. By employing the "withholding affection" technique as a deadly weapon, the poor man doesn't stand a chance. A new (ish) car is usually acquired in no time. As she is used to getting what she wants her priorities will always take precedence over everyone else's. This in part is what makes her so dangerous **any day** of the working week, but particularly in the mornings. She will always be late.

Alcohol fuelled Friday/ Saturday nights are spent covered in fake tan preening, pouting, , reapplying make-up and comparing herself to other Daddy's Little Girl's. Like a spider setting a web for an unsuspecting fly[4] she will (ironically) be hypersensitive to any bloke that shows the remotest interest in a 360 degree radius.

---

[3] Daddy's Little Girl is self aware and realises that she would not be in with a shout at nailing Justin, Ed on the other hand ...

[4] This is usually Rude Boy or Hi Viz Vest Man in training (see later chapters)

This is good news as Daddy's Little Girl spends Sunday (a high accident day for bikes) recovering as she is usually too delicate to go out on the road. This also means on a Monday she should be relatively sober. However, some Daddy's Little Girls are born with a face like the front of an Austin Allegro that no amount of fake tan or San Miguel can fix. These girls don't go out Saturday nights; they are too busy eating cake. This means that there is a chance they will be out on Sundays' but it is more likely to be on horseback, which presents its own challenges and not just for the horse (see Horse Woman later).

Predictability

Although completely unpredictable, there is some more good news. As Daddy's Little Girl's car is newish both brake lights will be working and the brake pads will have some wear left on them. However, the brakes are only applied (very forcibly) when she is 1 inch away from the car in front, the rest of the travelling time is spent answering a "what's app" message from her mate Stacey. Her predictability outside of this is zero and Daddy's Little Girl has a 5* danger rating for this reason.

Biker Response

To get past Daddy's Little Girl, leave at least two lanes of traffic between you and her. Steady progress by her is no indication of what might happen next. If she is in the middle lane of a motorway (normally is), this can be a problem. Approach slowly and do not dwell in her blind spot. Drop a gear to increase engine sound (Usually futile with the headphones in, but you can accelerate faster). Hopefully your full beam will already be on having spotted the frustrated ambulance driver ahead.

Always leave a good gap. Daddy's Little Girl will at some point look down to switch over the playlist from Ed to Justin during brief spells of disillusionment[3], and suddenly notice the traffic has stopped to let the ambulance through.

Watch out for other Daddy's Little Girl's on the prowl. If one notices there is a gap in front of you, she will be in there and that prawn sandwich will be history.

Hi-Viz Vest Man

The table below sets out what to look for. Please read on to understand the man.

How to identify

Parameters	What to expect
Driver Age Range	25-39
Typical Car/ Van	10 years old + Vauxhall Cavalier/Escort Van billowing diesel
Colour	White if a van, blue /dull colour if a car and not washed for weeks
Driving Style	Fast and prone to lane drift, sticks to the middle lane. Tends not to change lanes quickly
Tell-tale signs	Driver window down (whatever the weather) elbow resting on the side, puffs of smoke/flicks of ash hitting the visor.
Danger Rating	***

The comments below do not refer to the everyday Hi-Viz Vest Man going about his daily business. They are directed at those that are not paying attention when driving or do not think it is important to look after their machinery.

Hi Viz Vest Man is not a danger as such (it is always a bloke) it is the vehicles they tend to drive. Features to expect include:-

- One or both brake lights to be non-functioning
- Tyres will be worn to the limit on at least 3 corners. There will be one recently refurbished cross ply on at the back with no hubcap cover
- Neither the car and most certainly not the van would have been serviced for at least 5 years

- The vehicle will definitely pull to one side when Hi-Viz Vest Man takes both his hands off the wheel to light his next fag[5].

Personality Type

You have to remember which day of the week it is with these guys. Monday morning is the most dangerous time. Sunday night they would have been down the Fox and Hounds or the local working men's club having got completely rat arsed and may not be operating on all cylinders.

It is not their fault. The prospect of another week of mind numbing tedium standing by a set of roadworks in all weathers having to listen to a power crazed short-arsed tarmac toting tosspot would piss anyone off. For the most part these guys are aware of bikers or are indeed bikers themselves. They will all know someone that has been killed on a motorbike.

One of the reasons why some Hi-Viz Vest Men who drive cars (as opposed to vans) don't take off their vests, or leave it on the back shelf is to try and make the driver in front think they are in fact the police. Unfortunately this charade gets blown away by the failed catalytic converter and clouds of diesel fumes emanating from the exhaust, visible for miles; Apache Indians, if they were around, would start to prepare for war. Some have ended up wearing a vest as it is part of their company's policy. I have no problem with these people, just the w8nkers where you can see it was a deliberate ploy.

For the most part these men are hard working, devoted to their wife and children and always listen to "Talk Sport" radio; all have such a depth of knowledge of football and how to apply it, only Brian Clough at his best would surpass them[6]. If their team has lost on Saturday, it is only because

[5] For any of my American readers, "Fag" is English slang for cigarette.
[6] I am being sarcastic. Brian Clough knew more about football than most of us ever will just after being able to say "Dad da" and munching through his first Farleys rusk. It is just a fact.

they were not present at team selection and in the dugout to advise. Luckily they can phone up Talk Sport to let us know how they would have done it.

Home Life

Everyone struggles to meet bills from time to time and I have the deepest sympathy for all families where things are a bit tight. However, from a purely selfish biker's point of view, where the priorities (in order) are cigarettes, alcohol, the Sky TV subscription and the football season ticket, I get fed up. It is biker's lives that are put at risk because brake light repairs and service visits are too far down the priority list to be considered.

Predictability

As noted in the quick reference table above, the driver's window is always down, even if it is snowing. This is a good thing as usually they can hear you coming and do not have to rely on the side mirror that is usually cracked or missing. The danger element for Hi-Viz Vest Man comes when they are between fags or checking out the latest post from their mate "Dave" on their mobile phone. This is because the rigours of the days graft on Hi-Viz Vest Man's hands stops the circuit being made to get a response from the smartphone screen. As a result both hands can be off the wheel for some time and the one good tyre causes the van to drift. They are not watching what is in front at all. This can result in very sharp braking when they look up and suddenly notice the M62 has come to a halt or the overhead gantry actually has speed cameras fitted.

If you notice a Porsche Boxster, Mercedes SLK, Range Rover Evoque near Hi-Viz Vest Man, watch out. The chances are these cars will probably contain Exec Woman (See later) or some other attractive looking female who regularly does yoga[7]. There is no way he is not giving her an eyeful. When Hi-Viz Vest Man manages to tear his eyes away,

---

[7] It is a phenomenon that what some people consider non-attractive females, living at a home with no lock on the cake tin, do not usually drive these type of cars.

there is a sudden squealing of brakes as he notices the M62 has come to a halt or the overhead gantry actually has a speed camera fitted.

<u>Biker Response</u>

Depends what day it is and what the weather is like. Monday, give them a wide berth. Wait for the puffs of smoke or feel the ash hitting the visor before making your move it is at this point both hands are on the wheel. If it is raining, and you are in a blind spot, a short friendly blast of the horn is usually understood to let you get past.

Generally speaking I have found these guys to be respectful and aware of the biker. If you do get chance to speak to a Hi-Viz Vest man at the lights make sure you recommend a using a good nail brush and let him know one of his back lights are out. At least he will be able to answer the phone quicker. Who knows, he may get the rear light fixed instead of going to the match, especially if the manager is still playing a four-four-two formation and not heard his advice on Talk Sport to play three at the back.

Rude Boy

The table below sets out what to look for. These are bad boys, read on.

How to identify

Parameters	What to expect
Driver Age Range	21-26
Typical Car	Golf 2.0 Litre GTI , Mercedes A series sport
Colour	Golf Black; Mercedes White; tinted windows on either
Driving Style	Wears a baseball cap and sits too low in the seat
Tell-tale signs	Sports wheels, lowered chassis, sports styling, very high speed
Danger Rating	****

Rude boys are legends in their own imagination and have watched Fast and Furious 1, 2, 3, 4, 5, 6 and 7, twice. The incredible non-skill of being able to push an accelerator down to the floor on a 2 litre car seems to have taken a special significance for these testosterone filled little tinkers.

Personality Type

For some reason these guys wear sunglasses whether the sun is shining or not and sport a baseball cap even though they are inside a car with the roof up. They will of course smoke something, have no girlfriend and say "innit" and "blood" a lot.

They sit so low in their seat they can just see over the steering wheel. I have a theory that some think it will lower the wind resistance when they are driving fast. I think the others only do it as a means to get the appropriate purchase to waggle their jeans back up over their bottom, from the usual position of halfway up the back of their legs; it was safety pins through your nose in my day so I'm saying nothing. They throw litter (usually Maccy D's) out of their cars, anywhere.

Rude Boys like to think that they are untouchable and were always "too cool for school". This generates its own problems looking for work. However, they are great at marketing fast food chain produce in car parks and keep Sports Direct, Halfords and the children's jeans department of H&M busy.

Rude Boys who have passed any GCSE's are known as "Professors" and spend their spare time cultivating a confident "swagger style" of a walk to try and interest Daddy's Little Girl. For those who can find work, it is in a garage, warehouse or on a building site. This usually involves making tea, passing a left handed screwdriver, getting a glass hammer, being sent to buy a tin of tartan paint or going for a long stand. This means most of these little tykes get bored and drive fast to get some excitement.

Home Life

Evenings are spent in various country car parks or lay-bys away from prying eyes with other Rude Boys. The gathering is usually a customised mix of Vauxhall Corsas, Seat Leon Cupras or Peugeot 208s. They all have big exhausts, have no girls in them and piles of McDonalds packaging by the passenger and driver windows.

Their parents[8] have the same sense of social responsibility for their offspring as Tiddles (the cat next door) does when he is leaving his calling card on the lawn. In fact, in many ways all this is Tiddles' fault. He hangs out at night, trying to catch birds, thinks he looks cool and can leave piles of sh*t wherever he likes. He then goes home in the small hours and is fed and kept warm by showing his arse to the people he lives with. I don't blame Rude Boy for adopting this approach at all.

There are a few who are genuinely interested in cars and enjoy customising them and are really skilled. However, these kids know the limitations of their cars and do not want to risk damaging the

---

[8] Some parents of Rude Boy are fantastic. Unfortunately, there are people who are just born bad 'uns; no amount of nurturing will change it.

considerable investment their parents have made on undercar lighting and spoilers. Generally speaking these lads keep out of the way of bikers.

There are others though, who go out on the roads as high as a kite. These dudes are a serious danger and will do 120MPH + on the motorway or an A road. There is very little time to react. Even Tiddles with a pair 12 volt battery leads attached to his bollocks would struggle to react in time.

Biker Response

The biggest dilemma faced on two wheels if a car is coming up behind you at 120 plus is, do you pull into the inside lane or stay where you are? I wish I could tell you. All I can do is wish you well. Do not follow him. He will be in jail soon getting fu*ked regularly by "Harry the Spider" and end up with an arseh*le like a blood orange. At least I hope so.

Exec Man

The table below sets out what to look for. These are a growing breed and of course, the comments below only apply to those who drive like lunatics! Read on.

How to identify

Parameters	What to expect
Driver Age Range	Mid 30's – 40's
Typical Car	Audi A5 , BMW 4 - 6 Series, Range Rover
Colour	Black (Sports Styling), BMW's tend to be blue, Range Rovers black or white
Driving Style	Aggressive
Tell-tale signs	White shirt, cocky self important expression, stressed, tailgating everybody.
Danger Rating – Mellow Exec Man	***
Danger Rating – Normal Exec Man	****

Exec Man is a road bully. He is used to getting his own way at home and at work. Unfortunately he does not see the road any differently. Exec Man's specialism is tailgating and will try to force people out of his way, flashing his lights and throwing up his arms like you have done something wrong! He will be prone to sudden braking as well. These knob heads put their foot down (hard) to eat up any road space in front of them, no matter how short the distance.

As far as the tailgating and flashing lights are concerned I have observed it actually doesn't matter what speed you are doing. Even if you are going above the national speed limit he can't help himself. Only Rude Boy is likely to avoid being tailgated. Even Exec Man will not do 120MPH plus.

I have tried to understand why Exec Man feels the need to behave like this. In the narrative below I have set out a rationale in a bid to make sure that I am able to keep my own cool and get the f@*k out of his way.

Personality Type

He is turned on by power and control. When he arrives at work in the morning Exec man will hyped-up, stressed but slightly full of himself, having breakfasted on control toast and bullied eggs.

He is academically educated but with the same social skills and empathy as a schizophrenic moth with hearing difficulty and a limp. He will spend the day playing power politics, undermining and backstabbing others and setting unreasonable demands on work colleagues. He will be even worse by the time he gets home. Driving 6 inches from the car in front is highly stressful and this will not be switched off as he pulls into his driveway. My theory is that some people turn out like this when they want something as a child and they scream until mummy gives in. However, in this case I am more inclined to think that some people are just born arseh*les[9].

Home Life

There is no doubt about it, these guys have two mirrors in their hallways, a trophy wife who is living in utter misery with this self obsessed, power hungry, egomaniac. Exec Man is more concerned about showing his other middle class mates what material things he has got, rather than spending time showing his family how much they are loved and doing those "little things" for his wife. In conversation the only opinion that really counts is his and becomes aggressive or sulks if anyone dares to disagree.

His wife is the person I feel sorry for. Living with a narcissist domineering personality can be soul destroying. She will in all likelihood have had a career of her own but now works part-time having sacrificed that a long time ago for him.

---

[9]Examples can also be found on some commuter trains into London Euston.

The home of course will be immaculate and soulless. The poor woman would have learned to walk on egg shells around him. Any affection she shows is reserved for the family cat, Tiddles. Their sex life has dwindled to once a month on a Saturday night when her love starved muff that is normally as dry as the Atacama Desert, is caught off guard by the numbing effect of 5 double gins.

There is some good news if you are on a bike on Sunday. If Exec Man has managed to have sex with his comatose wife he will be less stressed for his trip to the golf club; at this point he turns into "Mellow" Exec Man for a short period of time. If he hasn't been laid please watch out. The sperm filled Exec Man has a 4* danger rating on Sunday.

Biker Response

Get out of the way as quickly as possible. Exec Man will think nothing of undertaking, or keeping his front bumper six inches behind you. Keep a safe distance when he overtakes, don't race him. I know we could all leave him for dead but believe me there is no better feeling than filtering past him as he sits stuck, fuming, in the next queue.

As tempting as it may be, avoid any sign language. Snatch that moral high ground and keep both hands on the handlebars. Pulling up along-side him and giving him "the stare" especially in a tinted helmet can help make you feel better. Following him to work if you have the time may make him think twice about tailgating bikers but I doubt it.

Speaking personally, I think giving him a good smack in the mouth[10] to make up for his mothers failings would make the world a nicer place and save someone's life one day.

---

[10] It is illegal to do this. Even in Wakefield.

Hi Boys... would you like a ride ?

Exec Woman

Parameters	What to expect
Driver Age Range	Mid 30's - early 50's
Typical Car	Audi A4 , Range Rover Evoque , Volvo, Audi Q
Colour	White (Sports Styling), Range Rovers Evoque in white, Volvo in white, Audi Q in white.
Driving Style	Passive aggressive
Tell-tale signs	Driver is groomed, smart , made up , slim, not unattractive
Danger Rating	**

Exec Woman is an increasing phenomenon and from a bikers point of view this is a good thing. She is generally far less aggressive than Exec Man but there is a problem. She was born a woman.

Just as women are coming to the end of the monthly reproductive cycle and associated hormone changes, there's the f*&king menopause. I'm glad I am a bloke.

These chemical shifts cannot be controlled by any woman. They have been trying ever since Eve noticed she was naked and suddenly wanted a fig leaf. It is just a force of nature and it changes some thoroughly decent human beings into homicidal maniacs[11]. This can lead to irrational decisions and aggressive tendencies. Never cross, gesture or do anything when Exec Woman in this mode.

Personality Type

She takes great pride in her appearance, wants to be treated with respect and be seen to compete on a better level than men. For some, this can lead to a cold and slightly prickly demeanour, adopting male posturing

[11] This of course does not apply to all women!

instead of using her femininity. Ok, Ok I mean she wears a trouser suit instead of a skirt. Make no mistake she has a strong personality, a sharp intellect and can drink neat gin.

Home Life

She is the main breadwinner and works hard and late, often at weekends. The sex life with her partner is limited to Saturday night, but only after she has had a "success" at work in the week. She may live alone but is probably married to Exec Man (See Exec Man home life for further details).The offspring, may well be a "Daddy's Little Girl" if female. Any males will probably be students, living away from home, only making contact when the washing basket is getting a bit high or the money is running a bit low.

Biker Response

It can be very difficult to judge. Exec woman is normally quite safe and a passive road user. They tend not to look out for bikers as they are too busy thinking about how to impress at the next meeting, what to make for tea, getting a parking space at work and another million things. If she is wearing her hair up it indicates she may be "on-one" get out of the way! Do not make any gesture at her or react in any way if there are any unexpected road manoeuvres, ever. Just ride on.

He's on his way.....

White Van Man

We all know him and what to expect but what is the story behind this character? Read on my friend.

Parameters	What to expect
Driver Age Range	20's – 28s
Typical Van	Ford Transit, Vauxhall Movano
Colour	White, but can be any colour if boxed shaped and not owned by the driver.
Driving Style	Aggressive, Fast
Tell-tale signs	Outside lane, tailgating, broken mirrors, dents
Danger Rating	***

It's the attitude with White Van Man and to be clear, I only mean the ones that drive like idiots. It is my theory that suppressed feelings of frustration with other aspects of his life turn him into a knob head on the road. It is only a theory.

The situation is worse when he has two of his knob head mates with him. The flasks propped up on the dashboard, the empty, semi-aggressive expressions peering out of the window. The van itself usually has rust spots and the odd scrape. The inside mirror is missing and as usual, only one of the brake lights will be working .Where the van is rented, this usually means the driver is not so used to driving on his side mirrors. The dangers are obvious.

There are some excellent considerate drivers of these vehicles, despite appearances. The made up comments below do not apply to these people.

Personality type

Whether the van itself is rented or part of a business one thing is for sure, it is not owned by White Van Man. This is the start of the problem. The "respect for others function" in the dark recesses and partially formed synapses of his brain has not had chance to fully develop. I think the logic goes something like; it is not my van, not my cost, not my company, not my insurance and therefore not my problem. Genius.

As a reaction to the frustrations he faces with life, White Van Man will attempt to show he is in control and a superior being behind the wheel. He dare take risks, his reactions are quicker; he is stronger, more powerful and better able to anticipate the behaviours of all around him. He cannot stop himself from tailgating. In his case it is not a bullying action like Exec Man, it is more a "show- off" I am better type thing. He is usually single and needs to get laid more than Exec Man. Unfortunately, he has the social graces of a baboon that has just been pissed on from a great height by a herd of elephants, after a particularly long day at the waterhole.

Home Life

Further feelings of resentment build up because he still lives at home and is subject to the rules of his parents house; this includes doing his own washing. Of course, this means he only changes his underpants every other day whether they pass the "sniff test" or not. Through no fault of his own, his employers business is struggling and it is generally late with tax payments to the Inland Revenue and the payment of wages to the White Van Men on its payroll. Van maintenance for the company is a luxury; the van itself can be as battered as the driver's pride. No wonder frustrations boil over. As I said, it is only a theory.

I would have more sympathy but this dude puts lives at risk and can also scare Daddy's Little Girl or a member of the Wrinkly Brigade into doing something stupid as we go past.

Biker Response

First check if both mirrors on the van are broken or missing completely. Be prepared for neither brake light to work. Expect sudden braking, as the van will be tailgating a member of the Wrinkly Brigade, especially if they are in the middle lane. Do not undertake this vehicle. Never overtake this character when approaching a feeder lane onto the motorway, without leaving at least two lanes clear. Get by fast. Once they are aware of you they will let you past. Also it is unusual to see him out on a Sunday.

The good news is that White Van Man will be interested in bikes and may be a biker himself and stop to chat. Always suggest a multi pack of new underpants for Christmas, if he asks; you can get 10% discount.

The Wrinkly Brigade

Parameters	What to expect
Driver Age Range	65+
Typical Car	Ford Fiesta, Fiat Ford Focus, Austin Allegro, anything "Vander Plas"
Colour	Beige
Driving Style	Slow
Tell-tale signs	Hunched 1 inch away from the steering wheel, no signals, alone in the middle lane
Danger Rating	**
Danger Rating at Junctions	*****

The plus point with the Wrinkly Brigade is that their eyesight is so poor (generally speaking)[12] they cannot read a mobile phone when driving (or at any other time). Bluetooth, tends to be a complete mystery so there are not too many knobs and switches to get confused over if they do get a call when driving.

The only concern for this driver is for the next toilet stop.

There are some brilliant older drivers. Any comments below do not represent these people. As with this whole book its purpose is to keep bikers alive. (None of this applies to anyone I know, especially you mum).

Personality type

These people are not in a hurry... anywhere. They have realised their life is hurtling toward an appointment at the pearly gates and the only speed bumps they have is watching episodes of Countdown and Bargain Hunt

---

[12] Age-related conditions include macular degeneration, cataract, diabetic eye disease, glaucoma, low vision and dry eye.

during the day, so they take their time over everything. This includes making cups of tea, drawing the curtains and paying for anything in shops. Unfortunately this also extends to the car indicator lever. Do not expect any signals but a slow drift that could be one way or the other[13].

Home Life

I imagine that most of the day, outside of Bargain Hunt and Countdown, is spent looking out of the window and waiting for the children and grandchildren to turn up for some money. For the less active, who are not members of a church or a U3A (University of the Third Age), the other priorities are Coronation Street or East Enders[14], a nice cup of tea and a nice drive out on Sundays. And there is the problem.

Biker response

As already mentioned (too many times) there are a high proportion of accidents involving bikers on a Sunday. Typically, there are of course more bikers out on a weekend, but there is also a much higher proportion of the Wrinkly Brigade.

It is not the individual brigade members that actually present a danger. It is all the other car drivers frantically trying to get around them on the minor/A roads. They will almost certainly be in the middle lane of a motorway, if they dare go on one.

If it were the African plains, rather than the M62, Exec man would take them down like a lion hunting a blind gazelle with "Please come and eat me" branded on its side. If Rude Boy is still up from Saturday night he will be revving furiously, stereo pumping, pupils dilated looking for half an inch of road to get past (Daddy's Little Girl, Exec Woman, Hi-Viz Vest Man, White Van Man will still be in bed).

One of the mysteries I have never solved is why the Wrinkly Brigade drive at that annoyingly slow speed and then suddenly speed up

---

[13] Obviously this not the case with everyone! (See disclaimer)

[14] It is always one or the other. East Enders is usually watched by the depressed ones thinking of booking a trip to Switzerland.

whenever it is safe to overtake. I would love to think they do it deliberately. This can cause frustration and some bikers to take unnecessary risks. Patience is the order of the day.

However, please remember if a rampant Exec man is behind you or a "Jesus" (See next chapter); make sure you do your lifesavers. They won't wait for you to make a move in slow moving traffic!

Watch out for any public conveniences coming up if you are stuck behind the Wrinkly Brigade. Expect sudden braking and sharp turns left or right (no indication obviously) depending on what side of the road the toilets are on.

Every biker knows to expect people to pull out at junctions. If the Wrinkly Brigade are about to pull out, it is my hypothesis that the danger is massively exaggerated because of the eye conditions noted above[12]. If you don't have time for evasive action before you are T boned[15], I would recommend the following measures. As you are flying through the air to make your appointment with the tarmac, say a prayer to the almighty, be glad you put clean undies on that morning, bless your children and try to forgive the driver for saying "Sorry, I just didn't see you". That makes it all alright, doesn't it.

---

[15] Where bikes of all kinds crash into the front side of a car as the driver pulls out of a junction without looking properly. It is a crash at right angles, forming a letter T.

Jesus'

Fellow bikers who damn well ought to know better.

Parameters	What to expect
Biker Age Range	21-33 – (There are no Jesus' alive over 33)
Typical Bike	Ninja, R1
Colour	Green
Riding Style	Aggressive
Tell-tale signs	Swerving in and out of traffic at very high speeds. Tailgating cars, not giving "The Nod" to other bikers
Danger Rating	*****

There you are looking out for Exec Man screaming up behind you, Daddy's Little Girl swerving in front of you , Hi -Viz Vest Man decelerating through the clouds of diesel fumes, the insane antics of Rude Boy and one of our own decides to ride like a tw*t.

It was reinforced no end of times by my instructor when I was training to pass my bike test years ago to do my "life savers"[16]. This simple act has saved a number of tarmac surfing sessions following encounters with Rude Boy in particular and, I am dismayed to say, with Jesus'.

All bikers from time to time open up the throttle. Most however, wait for clear roads and do not scream up behind other bikers. This bloke is on a sports bike and has been on one track day and thinks he is Barry Sheen/ Foggy/ The Doctor/ Shakey Byrne (depending on your age). Somehow, other bikers have become competitors.

This moron thinks he has been granted the divine gift of being able to see into the future and anticipate every eventuality. If brains were taxed

---

[16] This is the quick glance over the shoulder left or right before making a manoeuvre on a bike.

distressing or damaging others. They live in the moment and are grateful for what they have.

Home Life

Happily married, living a stress free peaceful life. They are at ease with themselves and have a wonderful network of friends and family. They are respected and loved in the community. They are also often involved in charity work and attend car boot sales with the dog called Muffin. Muffin spends his days barking at Tiddles crapping on their lawn when they are at work.

Biker Response

Slowly ease your throttle back as they signal left and politely pull over and let you get on your way. The appropriate response is a small hand gesture, on the clutch side, acknowledging their angelic status. Whisper a prayer of thanks to the bikers Gods and bless the Angel's family. Burn on.

Lorry Drivers

Parameters	What to expect
Age Range	30- 57
Typical Vehicle	18 Wheeler, container
Driving Style	Too close to the vehicle in front. Convoy with other wagons/lorries
Tell-tale signs	Country of ID plate is non-UK .White Registration Plate. Foreign Logos.
Danger Rating UKLID	**
Danger Rating PEES	****

Sorry, but the key question here is identifying if they are UK drivers (UKLIDS) or European (PEES). Specifically, are the PEES from countries that were at one time under communist rule?

In my experience the UK Lorry driver is very much aware of bikes and often makes allowances. However, there are some deadly situations.

One in particular is when there is a convoy of lorries on the inside lane of a motorway approaching a feeder road, I have noticed the UKLIDS often pull out into the middle lane some distance before. I have not noticed PEES do this.

In convoy, the PEES will decelerate when approaching a junction. This has a knock on effect on the other drivers as they have to brake or sharply pull into the next lane. The problem here is that if Daddy's Little Girl, Exec Man or Rude Boy is in this lane they will instantly move out into the outside lane (if on a motorway) so they are not stuck behind the lorry. They will not look behind them. The Wrinkly Brigade in the middle lane will not move and as a result there will be screeching of brakes and horns going off. The statistics show motorway casualties are relatively low but the same principle applies to dual carriageways and other "A" roads; only this time there is nowhere to go.

Eastern Block

To drive a lorry in the UK the tests are tough. I have every respect for the lorry drivers of this country. They are highly skilled and understand that driving like a knob will leave them unable to provide for their families. From the statistical analysis section there are far fewer accidents involving HGV's as a percentage of licensed vehicles on the road.

There is a problem with the foreign lorry drivers though. In part there is the language barrier and the understanding of the highway-code and signage on the road. Many are perfectly capable and superb drivers. However, it would be utterly crass to say this is the case with everyone. Death is not racist. I don't care where you come from, what colour your skin is but if you cannot understand or are slow at interpreting instructions you are a danger to bikers.

This not just me being a right-wing nutter, by the way. Alright, it was a Daily Mail article published on 7th May 2015 that showed motorway accidents involving foreign lorries have soared by 14 percent (929 in 2012 to 1,061 in 2014) with Polish drivers topping the crash league table.[19] However, it is interesting to note that a third of accidents involving foreign lorries take place on motorways. I was not able to source statistics for A roads; shame.

---

[19] Source: the Accident Exchange – Published Daily Mail 7th May 2015

Biker Response

When Exec Man or Daddy's Little Girl are trapped behind a lorry approaching a feeder road then this is a highly dangerous situation of the biker. There are a couple of options.

One is to back off until the traffic in front has managed to sort itself out. The better option is to get into the outside lane (on a motorway) anticipating that this will happen. Leave a gap for Exec Man and Daddy's Little Girl to pull into. Believe me they will take advantage of it. You will not have time to get out of their blind spot, as I said they won't look behind them anyway.

On an A road look a long way in front watching out for these lanes and adjust your speed and position so there is plenty of empty gravel around you.

The good thing about big lorries is that if it is windy, especially if it is gusty you could do worse than use them as a buffer against the wind[20]. I know some bikers do this.

---

[20] Windy Hill (just as you descend after going across Saddleworth Moor) across the M62 has very sudden strong gusts from the side. Keep your body low against the tank when it's like this.

Cyclops Cyclists

Parameters	What to expect
Age Range	25- 57
Bike type	Road Bikes
Bike Type	Mountain Bikes
Riding Style	Two Abreast (one tit next to another)
Tell-tale signs	Long line of queuing traffic
Danger Rating	**

One of the saddest sights on the road, especially on an A road is the cyclist that thinks it is OK to ride two abreast, whatever is behind them. It is always on a Sunday morning[21]. It would not matter if the wife of the driver stuck behind this dynamic duo is 4cm dilated and screaming in agony. It does not matter the Wrinkly Brigade are late for church or Exec Man is going to miss tee off at the golf club and is already p*ssed off at being held up by the Wrinklies in the first place. It is not even a consideration that Jesus is trying to break the Isle of Man TT record for this stretch of road.

None of this is as important as the conversation that Batman and Robin are having about potholes and different f*cking types of lycra. I have long thought a small mirror on the handlebars so these guys can see the trail of misery behind them, would be a good idea.

[21] There are of course some very considerate cyclists out there training for all sorts and this narrative does not apply to them.

Personality Type

The riders tend to be optimistic but ultimately selfish people who will do "what they want"; even worse, they don't even realise that wearing lycra over a certain weight and age is a crime against humanity. They just can't see it. Road wise, they have the same sense of self preservation as a three legged rabbit asking for directions to the annual foxes brush convention.

Home Life

The reason these guys are out early Sunday morning is they have no-where to go on a Saturday night; certainly none of the pubs in Yorkshire tolerates idle chat about bottom chaffing in middle aged men. Instead of listening to Steve Wright's "Sunday Love Songs"[22], making a sausage roll with the wife, devouring a "Full English" and reading the sports section of the Sunday papers, they are out playing on their bikes. Their names are Trevor, Roger or "Pete". The truth is that they will outlive us all.

Biker Response

Obviously as a biker you would be making steady progress along the outside of the traffic queue created by the above named gentlemen, getting in between the gaps of traffic as the need arises. There will of course, be the odd car trying to stop you by pulling out as far as possible. It is also likely you will meet a car coming the other way frantically flashing their lights and driving directly at you to "make a point". It is likely to be a "Wrinkly" by the way, who fought in the war with a touch of Alzheimers going the wrong way to church.

Eventually you will arrive at the front of the traffic right behind the two oblivious cyclists still discussing chaffing, the relative merits of carrying a tyre repair kit or a full inner tube and are still on the subject of potholes.

---

[22] Love the show Steve, should you ever read this.. (no , I don't really think you ever will either)

Most cyclist move to single file when they hear a powerful motorbike behind them, for one of two reasons:-

1. They can no longer hear what the answer is to the inner tube question or
2. It could be a member of one of the fine motorbike clubs in the UK. Some are friendlier than others.

If they do not pull over immediately a couple of quick revs to increase the volume, just in case they have super power hearing, usually does the trick.

Please be very careful at this point, if Exec Man or (Unlikely but could be Rude Boy) are in the first three cars they will pull out and go for it and try and overtake you. They can't help it. If this happens back off immediately. There will be another queue a mile or two up the road. As I said, nothing feels better than sticking it to Exec Man.

Horse Woman

Horse Woman is often the female partner of a Cyclops Cyclists or the wife of Exec Man; Cyclops and Exec Man were up early to either meet "Pete" in his lycra or make the four ball tee off time with Crispin, Jeremy and Jasper. Horse woman is out on the road as at least she will have something to ride on a Sunday morning.

The younger female riders accompanying Horse Woman are usually Daddy's Little Girl "Altos" that were not picked up from the nightclub or ones that had too much separation anxiety to be away from the cake tin for more than 2 hours to go out of an evening. I swear I have seen a horse straining under the reins, looking at me slightly embarrassed as if to say "Look I don't pick 'em. I'm not Red Rum you know. I could have been a champion, a real contender.... blah blah".

To be fair there are some similarities between Horse Woman and bikers. Both groups intermittently wear hi-viz vest, need overpriced protective hard hats and have fallen off their steed at one time or another.

It is true Horse Woman can cause similar problems to the cyclists, but there is a difference. They generally do not ride two abreast, they are very much aware and respectful of the traffic and I would rather look at the bottom of Horse Woman bobbing up and down in front of me than two overweight middle aged men. I appreciate that not everyone will agree, fair enough.

Personality Type

The women are wealthy, privileged, well groomed and polite. They are used to having money; this aristo type "does one's duty to one's husband/partner on a Saturday night[23]" and then gets on with mucking out the stables. I have never seen a man on a horse on the road.

Home Life

Days are filled with endless coffee mornings, charity functions, supervising the gardener, moaning about the British economy and gossiping about the neighbours. Radio 4 is on in the background at all times, except Sunday mornings.

Biker Response

You don't have to be Tonto to tell if Horse Woman may be further up the road. The steaming piles of horsesh*t [24] every 100 yards, the smell of the countryside and increased number of Range Rovers that actually look like they have been used off road, rather than just taking the kids to school are all good clues.

Horses are naturally more jumpy around motorbikes, so keep the revs down in a low gear and ride slowly and smoothly past giving them a wide berth. Nod to the rider, even if it is an "Alto" [25] on board. It is the right thing to do.

[23] The exception is the wife of Exec Man, where gin rather than a sense of duty is needed.

[24] Yep, lots of debate on the horse-shit issue for bikers. Not one I am going to discuss here.

[25] Alto is a made up term for those females who sing in the lower register and may need to shave regularly.

The Police

As can be seen in table 5 in chapter on "Deaths by Road User Types and Other Stuff" you are more likely to have an accident on an "A" road than any other type of road. For reference, the top ten dangerous roads in Britain are set out in the appendix.

It does seem logical that the resources spent to keep us safe should be re-directed to A roads, whether it is a police presence, better signage (i.e. feeder lanes), mending potholes or cameras on accident black spots rather than the motorways. Of course, motorcyclist should take responsibility as well and not ride beyond their abilities just to keep up with their mates.

When I talk about resources I am not referring to the "Safety Camera Partnership" by the way. I think it should be renamed to "Entrapment for the unwary motorist on sections of road where the speed limit is set far too low". It might mean buying longer vans to fit all the words on, but at least it would be a more accurate description.

The real source of the problem is the town councils that set the limits on these sections of roads in the first place and do not put up "repeater" signs.

The police know where these anomalies exist and target them. It seems so unfair when fixed cameras are painted bright yellow and can be seen a long way ahead so you can adjust in good time but somehow video vans can be covert.

I feel sorry for the policemen and women ordered to sit in these video vans surrounded by oxygen masks in case they choke on the rarefied air of the legal moral high ground.... or when they fart in that enclosed space.

Interceptors

Unless you are Jesus[26] the police tend to leave bikers alone. I have no complaints, other than I wish *any* camera footage of Exec Man, Rude Boy and Daddy's Little Girl's antics could be used to prosecute and get them off the road. Exec Man could learn to be nicer to his wife, Rude Boy could pick up his old Maccy D's packaging and Daddy's Little Girl could walk to the nightclub instead of driving and lose some lard. Win-win all round.

Biker Response

The entrapment areas represent a massive danger to bikers who may have to suddenly brake, due to cars suddenly braking in front.

Bikers do have an advantage of course over cars in this scenario as there is no number plate on the front of bikes It is so very tempting to give the one fingered salute on behalf of the rest of humanity to the police video van. Don't take it for two reasons.

1. You will have to take your hand off the handlebars and you are speeding.
2. Some professional tw*ts take binoculars into the van with them so they can read normal sized number plates when you go past. All's fair in love and war, take what cover you can as a precaution.

[26] See chapter on Jesus'.

Summary & Game for the Car

I really hope you have enjoyed reading this and found it useful. Good luck out there and I guarantee you will spot these characters on every journey you have. Please stay safe. I have set out a scoring system in the table below for the family to play on long trips. First to 100 points wins.

Ref:	Description	Danger Rating	Points
Daddy's Little Girl	Daddy's Little Girl	*****	10
Hi-Viz Vest Man	Hi-Viz Vest Man	***	5
RB	Rude Boy	****	20
Exec Man	Normal Exec Man	****	10
Exec Man	"Mellow" Exec Man	***	100
Exec Woman	Exec Woman	**	15
WVV	White Van Man	****	5
Jesus	Rogue Biker	*****	20
Angels	Angels	*	5
UKLids	UK Lorry Drivers	**	5
PEES	European Lorry Drivers	****	10

Special note for kids - automatic 20 bonus points awarded for any successful prediction of the next move for these characters make (includes tailgating)! No cheating – the car driver has the final say.

Other Basic Tips

1. Tyres
    a. Check the tyre pressure at least once a week and before any long journey
    b. Check for wear and any squaring off (Tyres are designed to lean over when cornering – if you have a long motorway commute the curve on your tyre will become flat. This causes handling problems especially going round bends)
    c. Make sure they are legal (1mm tread depth for a bike) continuously across 75% of the tyre. I wouldn't let them get that low with Daddy's Little Girl around. Get them changed at 2mm

2. Maintenance
    a. Always check your brakes, especially if it is raining. Some low speed braking helps get a feel of the grip of the road and the bikes behaviour before you get going.
    b. Always get your bike serviced as per the manual, or at the start of each new season
    c. Make sure the chain is sufficiently lubricated[27]
    d. Get heated grips fitted

3. Check the Weather
    a. Don't go out if it is going to be rainy, foggy or windy (i.e. above a wind speed of 14).If you have to go across windy hill on the M62 and its 14 + pack a spare pair of underpants.
    b. If it is gusty ride with your body flat across the tank and be ready for the gusts. (I stick my knee out into the wind

[27] Certainly more than Exec Man's wife

if it is coming from the side. It makes me feel better, though I have no idea if it is really effective!)

4. Gear
    a. Keep your visor clean
    b. Always wear the right protective gear whatever the weather
    c. Keep sunglasses in your side-bags, or use a legal sunscreen/ smoked visor. The police tend not to bother as long as these are used in bright daylight. If it is dark take the visor strip off. You will end up being part of the statistics included in here.
    d. Hi-viz vests, although compulsory in many countries, are not that trendy in the UK with bikers. I have read the arguments back and forth. My own view is anything that gets us noticed is a good thing. I personally draw the line at the Hi-viz vest that has the policing hatchings across it with "Polite" written on the back. It is hard not to think "w&nker" every time one passes me.

5. Road Hazards
    a. Avoid white lines, potholes, cracks in the road
    b. Don't corner over manhole covers
    c. Grit/ gravel – stay the f&*k away!
    d. Diesel on wet roads, usually on roundabouts

Appendix

The most dangerous routes have been ranked by the Road Safety Foundation. These are:-

1. A18: From Laceby to Ludborough, Lincolnshire
2. A36: From A3090 to Totton, Hampshire
3. A588: From A585 Blackpool to Lancaster
4. A44: From Llangurig to Aberystwyth
5. A532: From A530 to A534 Crewe, Cheshire
6. A291: From Canterbury to Herne Bay, Kent
7. A6: From M6 junction 33 to Lancaster
8. A361: From Chipping Norton to Banbury, Oxfordshire
9. A40: From M40 junction 5 to High Wycombe, Buckinghamshire
10. A643: From Brighouse to Morley, West Yorkshire

Source: The Road Safety Foundation

The End – Keep it shiny side up.

Printed in Great Britain
by Amazon